BUSINESS Rules!

BUSINESS
Rules!

52 ways you can achieve business success

written by **MICHAEL SANSOLO**

illustrated by **STEVE HICKNER**

BRIGANTINE MEDIA

Illustrations by Steve Hickner

Brigantine Media
211 North Avenue, St. Johnsbury, Vermont 05819
Phone: 802-751-8802 | Fax: 802-751-8804
Email: neil@brigantinemedia.com
Website: www.brigantinemedia.com

ISBN 978-1-9384064-0-9

Printed in Canada

Dedication

Janice, Sarah, Corey, Mom, and Dad—
thank you all for yesterday, today, and tomorrow

Acknowledgments

My great thanks go to all of those included in this book, who shared their insights, time, and honesty. The brevity of the chapters only hints at the wisdom each of them has to impart.

Thanks to Janis Raye and Neil Raphel, my publishers and editors, for asking me to write this book and whose guidance helped craft it. Thanks to Steve Hickner for his amazing illustrations. Thanks to my usual writing partner, Kevin Coupe, who finds a way to make every day interesting.

Special thanks to all those who make life matter: Robin, Marcy, Susan, Adam, Jack, Nat, David, and Jonathan; Kay, Larry, Den, Nancy, Cheryl, Sharon and Doug; Amy, Dennis, Elissa, Kelly, Kim, Kristin, Lauren, and Stephen; plus many other family members both human and canine.

Thank also to countless friends and, of course: Corey and Sarah for trying to teach me classical music and poetry, respectively; Mom and Dad for the foundation of everything; and Janice for her love, support, and cookies.

The Rules

The Rules

Start with the Golden Rule.

ALTHOUGH BUSINESS IS complex, the rules that guide us can be extremely simple. Bill Clinton first won the presidency with the famously simple message of "It's the economy, stupid." The motto of Google is "Don't be evil."

Rules play an important role. They give us discipline to keep our work on track and focus a team around the task at hand.

A century before Christ's birth, a man asked the prophet Hillel if all the wisdom of the Torah, the first five books of the Bible, could be explained by someone while standing on one foot.

Given this challenge, Hillel replied (probably on one foot): "What is hateful to you, do not do to your neighbor. That is the essence of the Torah; the rest is commentary."

It's the Golden Rule—treat others as you wish to be treated yourself.

Always remember to treat others—subordinates, colleagues, trading partners, and certainly, customers—the way *you* wish to be treated. There probably is no simpler way to achieve success.

Be distinct.

IT'S EASY TO be different, but it's not always a wise course of action. Driving on the wrong side of the street would be different, but it wouldn't achieve any goal aside from creating havoc.

It's far better to be *distinct*.

So many aspects of business are essentially the same. Airlines fly planes, retailers sell products, manufacturers build widgets. But in every field, there are companies that stand out by being distinct.

Southwest Airlines, for example, markets its distinctions, from the lack of baggage fees to the simple price structure to the offbeat nature of its staff. Progressive Insurance focuses on flexible pricing, Jimmy Johns sandwich shops on speed, and Hyundai on its extra-long warranties.

A company can be distinct in many ways: through service, products, prices, promotions, or even location. The best companies make their points of distinction so clear that even the most distracted consumer can name what makes them different. And those companies make sure every associate understands and serves that point of distinction.

That's what makes a winner.

Nothing beats a great attitude.

IN THE FIELD of thousands who competed in the 2014 Boston Marathon, Larry Chloupek stood alone.

It wasn't because Larry won; in fact, he didn't come close. Through each of the twenty-six miles of the course, Larry was greeted with thunderous applause for doing something most people could never imagine. He completed the Boston Marathon as the only entrant on crutches.

Larry lost his left leg to childhood cancer, but he has hardly lost anything since. Now in his fifties, Larry runs, golfs, bikes, and coaches countless teams, all on one strong leg and a pair of crutches.

Larry entered the Boston race to make a point to those injured in the bombing the previous year. He wanted to show that life goes on, races are entered, and the spirit endures.

Larry's effort reminds us that actions and deeds determine who you are, not the cards life has dealt you. Think about his lesson as you approach your job and your team. If you believe you can succeed, you will find a way. There are countless stories of famous people, from FDR to Stephen Hawking, who overcame physical and emotional handicaps to achieve great success.

In that way, Larry Chloupek—a friend of mine for the past decade—remains one of the most capable people I know. His attitude makes him able to do almost anything.

Support the whole team.

WHEN A CAPACITY crowd of 71,008 fills M&T Bank Stadium to root for their beloved Baltimore Ravens, they cheer for quarterback Joe Flacco or for the stout defense. No one thinks about Don Follett.

Don Follett is the director of fields for the Ravens. It's his job to make sure the team is always on sound footing. His goal is a field that lets the players do their best. Follett's handiwork goes unnoticed, and that's okay by him. Follett is invisible even though the game depends on him.

But someone in Baltimore understands the importance of Follett's role and all the other non-football-playing roles that have made the Ravens one of the most successful NFL teams for more than a decade. That person is the Ravens' owner, Steve Bisciotti.

Bisciotti's leadership style hasn't gone unnoticed.

Sportswriters frequently praise the entire Ravens' organization as one of the calmest and most professional in sports. Bisciotti lets the professionals in the organization do their jobs.

Follett says there's more. Bisciotti has built a spirit of oneness into the organization, making sure every employee is valued and connected. When the Ravens win big, the benefits find their way to everyone. That spirit ties everyone in the organization—in all those invisible jobs we never see, but could never watch a game without—to the success of the franchise.

It makes no difference to Follett that he will never see thousands of fans wearing his name on a jersey. He knows he's part of a winning team.

Focus on your best customers.

THERE IS A new force speaking to the power of customer loyalty, and her name is Lady Gaga.

Lady Gaga, known for her singing, dancing, and stunning wardrobe choices, is also a paragon of marketing for the electronic age. Jackie Huba, who co-authored the *Church of the Customer* blog, has studied and written extensively about Lady Gaga as a marketing genius.

Huba says the core of Gaga's strategy is to focus on her best customers—her one percent most engaged followers. By talking and listening to them largely through social media, Gaga makes them advocates of her brand. Their enthusiasm spreads to the rest of her followers, affectionately called her "Little Monsters."

This strategy has garnered her millions of fans worldwide.

By focusing on her most loyal followers, Gaga builds her strength. They share their passion to others, expanding her overall fan base and, in the process, expanding the numbers of her one percenters.

More businesses should go Gaga about their best customers.

Don't get too full of yourself.

WE ALL LIKE praise. We like to hear that we are smart or funny, that our haircut looks good or our clothing looks fashionable.

But businesses have to be careful not to get too carried away with praise. As many business leaders have cautioned me through the years, "Never breathe your own exhaust."

If you only breathe your own exhaust, you die, because your body can't use the carbon dioxide you exhale. If a company only listens to its own opinions and feedback, it can die, too. Companies that ignore outside voices struggle to see their own weaknesses and miss opportunities for improvement.

Sadly, there are countless examples of companies that were too insular in their focus: American automotive companies that missed the power of Asian competitors when they dismissed those cars as lesser quality; Kodak, the film company that invented and then walked away from digital photography.

Encourage other viewpoints. It could be like a breath of fresh air.

Ask for help.

MAYBE IT WAS because he was facing a life and death moment. Or maybe it was simply the product of a great management style.

At the most critical moment of his life, Chesley "Sully" Sullenberger asked the simplest possible question and demonstrated that there's no shame in asking for help.

Sullenberger, of course, is the pilot who safely landed a critically damaged jet in New York's Hudson River in January 2009, saving all the passengers in the process.

But there's more to the story. When the plane was only three hundred feet above the water, Sullenberger, as captured on the flight recorder, asked his crew a simple question. "Anyone have an idea?" he asked.

Sullenberger says that he had no expectations, but he knew the question needed asking. If anyone had an idea of how to restart the engines or best land on water, Sullenberger wanted to hear it. It wasn't a time to go through hierarchy. No one had a better idea, so Sullenberger continued with his gambit, and luckily, it worked.

Most businesspeople will never face a moment anywhere near as critical as Sullenberger's, but learn from his example. A leader has to be willing to both act and ask.

Plan for the worst.

HAS THIS EVER happened to you? You're running late for a flight or an appointment, but you hope everything will go your way and you will just make it on time. Then the breaks you need don't come—there's a traffic jam at the airport exit or you can't find a parking spot—and you are late.

Everything rarely goes our way, but too many businesses and business people act as if we'll get all the breaks. We build business plans, budgets, and strategies based on the unlikely occurrence that everything will go our way.

And we are shocked when things go awry.

Classical musicians have an interesting way of preparing for the worst case. They deliberately practice under poor conditions to hear their sound at its very worst. They seek out rooms with bad acoustics when they are getting ready for a performance.

By playing in the worst possible conditions, they force themselves to confront flaws and improve their playing. They know their sound will be infinitely better in the concert hall with warm and forgiving acoustics.

It's a great idea for business. Build strategies and tactics for the worst-case scenarios to help you focus on the core issues that you must get right.

Just think how well you'll perform when you catch a few breaks.

Retention begins on day one.

"THERE'S NEVER A second chance to make a first impression." That's doubly important when it comes to new associates. Like it or not, day one matters a lot.

One of great strengths of successful companies is a stable workforce. Lower turnover means that less expense and time is spent on recruiting and training. What's more, experienced employees have on-the-job knowledge that simply can't be taught. That's why many companies now look at measuring retention as well as turnover.

Human resources experts say a key step to building a strong and happy workforce starts on a new associate's first day. Managers need to learn how to give a proper orientation and make new hires feel they have signed up with the right company. Managers need to set clear objectives and high standards, and must remember to treat their workers with respect, solicit their feedback, and help them grow.

It all begins with that first day.

At one company where I worked, an employee council created the idea of new hire "buddies." The buddy's job focused on the basics, such as finding the bathrooms, the copy machines, the lunchroom, and giving a quick walking tour of the entire office. This simple idea gave each new hire a feeling of belonging right from the start.

Every great career begins on its first day.

Show up.

THERE'S A LOT any employee can learn from film director Woody Allen's quote: "Eighty percent of success is just showing up."

Certainly, just showing up doesn't guarantee anything, but it's an essential first step. Showing up is a great way to find opportunity, express interest, and get noticed. Sometimes it can be a key step on the path to making a real difference.

Consider the heavily publicized incident involving Nevada rancher Cliven Bundy. For many days in April 2014, Bundy's dispute with the Federal Bureau of Land Management over grazing fees for his cattle made him a media and political star. Despite all the publicity given Bundy, Adam Nagourney from the *New York Times* was the only reporter who personally showed up to witness Bundy's comments.

Bundy's celebrity ended when Nagourney wrote about the rancher's impromptu daily press conference, at which Bundy featured a diatribe against African Americans. The national media quickly changed its focus on the story.

You can learn a lot just by showing up.

Be five minutes early.

WRITING AN ADVICE column to new college graduates entering the working world, Michelle Singletary of the *Washington Post* had little trouble deciding on her first suggestion.

Show up on time!

It's advice that is so simple and yet so important. Employers and customers count on us for many things including value, quality, and consistency. But first they need to know when to expect us.

And since it's always best to give a little more, I amend Singletary's advice. Don't just be on time—be five minutes early. Showing up five minutes early is easy, and it demonstrates caring and commitment to your superiors and your customers.

Giving a little extra has fueled plenty of business success. Quicker than promised deliveries is the magic behind the "wow" factor Zappos gives its customers. Its shipments often arrive the morning after the order, well before they're promised.

Being early doesn't guarantee anything . . . except a head start to success.

Use your network.

THE OLD MAXIM was that it didn't matter *what* you knew, but *who* you knew.

In today's world of non-stop communication the rule has expanded. What matters is who you know and who those people know—your network.

In the past, reputations for goods, products, services, and people were spread by word of mouth. Today, word of mouth is enhanced by Yelp, TripAdvisor, Pinterest, and, of course, Facebook and Twitter.

Are you working your network? Joy Nicholas, a retail consultant based in Austin, Texas, sets aside time each week for connecting with her network. Through the Network of Executive Women, she fosters relationships with people who offer many different skill sets.

When a client needs help with a technology purchase, marketing, or human resources, Joy has a ready list of experts to contact. If a small retailer is looking for a new cash register system, Joy can reach out in her network to similar-sized operators to learn from their experiences, which helps her make better recommendations to her client.

Build your network. *What* you know always matters, but *who* you know can be even more valuable.

Create a better hiring process.

WHEN ANY CEO is asked to explain the strong performance of a company, the response is always the same: "Our people are the key to our success."

People really do make the difference. Companies should focus plenty of attention on the first step, the employee interview. But that process is rarely given much thought.

Mel Kleinman, president of Humetrics, a human resources consulting firm, says there are a few simple steps that make all the difference in hiring decisions.

Before looking for a new employee, decide if the job should be done differently—or at all. Then decide what type of person you want. If a new hire is overqualified, he or she is liable to become bored and leave. If the new staff member is less than qualified, work will suffer. You need to know what you want to hire correctly.

Before an interview, read the candidate's resume to prepare detailed questions. Ask for specific experiences, not strengths and weaknesses. (And give the candidate a chance to respond fully. In other words, listen.)

A better hiring process equals better employees and better company performance.

Spread the message.

IN 1962, PRESIDENT Kennedy was touring the NASA Space Center when he met a janitor carrying a broom. Kennedy asked the janitor what he was doing.

"Well, Mr. President, I'm helping to put a man on the moon."

There's a story of alignment. A leader, JFK, has set a clear and specific goal to put a man on the moon, and throughout the organization the task is clear. A janitor doesn't just clean; he is helping attain the goal.

Great leaders imbue their teams with that spirit of importance. David Dillon, the recently retired CEO of Kroger, took up blogging to spread his message to employees across the United States. His outreach from the top helped make clear that every job in the organization contributes to the company's mission.

More than ever, prospective employees understand the importance of company mission. Many use sites like GlassDoor.com to learn about the company culture, management style, and dedication to the mission. As GlassDoor's website exclaims: "Get hired. Love your job."

Rob Bell, a speaker and consultant on personnel issues, talks about his early career working in a supermarket. One morning during a raging snowstorm, his kids asked why he was venturing out to work. Bell summed it up beautifully.

"I'm going to feed the world."

As consumers of all kinds of goods and services, we count on that level of employee commitment. We count on mechanics properly fixing truck brakes. We count on baggage handlers moving millions of pieces of luggage from plane to plane. We count on supermarkets opening so we can get food after the snowstorm hits.

There are no small jobs when leadership makes the message clear.

Fail fast and fail cheap.

ONE OF THE most important skills to learn in many sports is how to fall. Take a class in self-defense or figure skating and you'll get instruction on how to fall correctly.

Businesses also need learn how to fall—or rather, how to fail. We know failure is going to happen. The key is learning to fail correctly.

New ideas are important, but companies must recognize that not everything works. The quicker an organization makes the call to end a failing project, the sooner the company will limit its investment in it and the quicker the turnaround to a new project.

When a project fails slowly, teams spend more

time and more resources. In the end, the failure is more costly, and the organization grows more risk averse because of those costs.

Failing fast and cheap doesn't inhibit innovation. It encourages businesses to keep moving, to keep hunting for ideas. If one idea doesn't work, maybe the next one will.

Measure yourself against the best.

IF A COMPANY wants to succeed it has to keep an eye on the best performers and match up with them. Nothing else will do.

Bob Bartels, the chairman of Martin's Super Markets in Indiana and Michigan, learned about the importance of competing with the best. His lesson was key to keeping his small family business growing for decades despite powerful competitors.

In the mid-1960s, Bartels was feeling great about how his stores had performed in the past year. Sales were up and the numbers were looking strong.

But one day Bartels got a cold dose of reality. A business colleague with insights from a much larger chain in the area gave him some shocking news: not a single one of Bartels's stores equaled the financial performance of the larger chain's worst store.

In other words, the good year really wasn't all that good when measured against strong competition.

Bartels still tells this story today because of the powerful lesson it packed. It motivated him to sharpen his company's focus and push performance to a level he didn't even think was possible. And that's probably why Martin's, unlike so many other family retailers, is still thriving.

Find your best competitors and benchmark them.

Don't make perfection the goal.

SHELLEY BROADER, THE president and CEO of Walmart in Europe, the Middle East, and Sub-Saharan Africa, has a saying: "Don't let perfection be the enemy of good."

Broader didn't create that idea. It dates back to both Aristotle and Confucius. (I never met either of the two philosophers, but I was lucky enough to work with Broader, so she gets to share the wisdom.)

The time, resources, and focus needed to get something all the way to perfect can become counterproductive. That same effort could move to another project and produce significantly more impact for an organization.

There's a fabulous example of this rule in wartime history. During the Battle of Britain in World War

II, an engineer created a rudimentary radar system for the Royal Air Force. He admitted the system wasn't perfect, but explained that even at eighty percent effectiveness it would and did help the British survive the onslaught.

It's similar to the way software is frequently released in semi-completed form, with users providing beta tests to improve it. Open-source software such as Linux is a great example of a product that has succeeded with just such a formula.

Granted, there are times when we want things to get as close to perfection as possible—landing an airplane or performing open-heart surgery. But in day-to-day business operations, getting things done is often more valuable than doing them perfectly.

That's wisdom you can use from Aristotle and Shelley Broader.

Add a little magic.

DESPITE ALL OUR education and years of experience, we can never, ever figure out a really good magic trick. We know magicians cannot possibly know what we are thinking, what card we just drew, or make a bowling ball appear out of thin air.

Yet they do it, and we are delighted.

Kevin Viner does comedy, illusions, and mind reading at corporate events, and his show is guaranteed to make you wonder. Viner says the key to a great trick is to keep the audience emotionally engaged by including the element of surprise. Even though everyone knows a trick is coming, they are still surprised when it happens because of the way Viner presents it.

Viner recognizes the power of emotional connection. Whether through jokes or his patter with the crowd, Viner knows his dialogue with the audience builds rapport, which builds connection. That, in turn, builds the energy of the entire room and leads to an exciting performance.

You've seen this at Disney World, where parading costumed characters distract children from the long lines for the rides. You see it at a savvy dentist office where they pump a pleasing aroma like fresh-brewed coffee into the waiting room to lessen patient anxiety.

Surprise, energy, connection, and humor do the trick.

Now you see it . . .

Quality is king.

YOU KNOW THE old joke—a tourist in New York asks, "How do you get to Carnegie Hall?" A jaded local responds: "Practice, practice, practice."

But ask Jeremy Handelman how to get to Broadway, and he says, "Quality, quality, quality."

Handelman, whose Off the Leash production company works on business videos and off-Broadway plays, says the challenge of making a theatrical production succeed is very similar to the challenge facing business in any field. You need quality.

Quality starts with an excellent script and a team that is passionate about the production. The producers need to know what will appeal to the audience and create a marketing campaign. Otherwise, a great production can disappear.

Like a Broadway production, business success relies on quality—you need a good product, a strong team, and a plan for success. All three.

A great product cannot overcome a poor marketing plan. Sales for Subway subs or Energizer batteries foundered until they found winning ad campaigns with Jared the weight-loss guy and the indefatigable bunny, respectively. And the best company reputation and sales staff won't save a poor product idea. Case in point: Harley-Davidson perfume.

At Krispy Kreme, a bad growth strategy almost sank the company until a new approach brought it back to life. The winning recipe—quality products, marketing, and management.

There's no business like show business? That's wrong. *Every* business is like show business.

Accept your business realities.

THERE'S AN OLD prayer about changing what can be changed, accepting what cannot, and knowing the difference. For many businesses, that's a key to success. If you fail to recognize the realities of your business, you can stray far from your customers' needs and expectations.

David Turk, the founder of Indiana Market and Catering in New York, has a keen sense of those limits. Turk knows the success of his business is providing clients the experience and peace of mind they want.

Catered food needs to travel to where it will be staged and consumed. So the measure of a great recipe is one that travels easily and both looks and tastes good when assembled, no matter how limited the kitchen capabilities or staffing at the destination.

Turk follows a simple model: "I prefer simple, fresh, and delicious food, transferable to the customer in a few easy steps. Our job is to make sure the clients can relax, knowing that we will never embarrass them and they have no fear of looking bad." He'll only try cutting-edge dishes when they mesh with the business model.

Understand your business realities—that's a recipe for success.

Turn your associates into engaged customers.

THERE ARE PROBABLY few jobs where execution matters more than military parachute packers. Although they work far behind the scenes and usually far from the front lines of battle, the packers perform a vital task.

Anyone who jumps out a plane—whether an Army Ranger or a first-time jumper—puts complete faith in the person who packed the chute. A tiny mistake can translate into disaster.

The military understands the importance of this role and has a unique and powerful way to ensure that the packers perform their jobs perfectly every time. Military parachute packers are required to make four jumps themselves each year. And on those jumps, their chutes are selected randomly.

That's a pretty solid way of getting top performance from everyone.

While businesses don't need to match the intensity of the military's policy, they can use the same rationale by turning staff into users.

It could be simple, such as a restaurant requiring servers to taste the food on the menu so they know what the customer will receive. Or it can be more complex, such as requiring doctors to spend time as patients to understand the care experience from that perspective.

Spending time in the customer's shoes can make you aware of important details. And you don't even have to jump out of a plane.

Move sideways to go forward.

THERE IS A reality to most careers and companies: only one person rises to the top. Most of the rest of us rise, but only so far.

And that doesn't have to be a bad thing.

One of the more interesting challenges in business currently comes in managing two immense generations: the baby boomers, now in their fifties and sixties, and the millennials, now in their twenties and thirties. With nearly 160 million people in the two groups, they challenge business leaders to understand how to use their talents and find ways to keep them engaged when sheer numbers dictate that upward mobility isn't universally possible.

The millennials are mastering the power of moving sideways as well as up. Inside an organization, that means taking a lateral job that requires different skills and provides new challenges.

Lateral moves broaden our skills and awareness, keep us engaged, and possibly make us more promotable in the future. What's more, lateral moves can help companies hang onto valued associates longer.

Early studies of the millennials suggest they are far less loyal to everything, including their employers. Sideways moves can help combat that trend, build skills, and move employees and companies forward.

Choose effectiveness over efficiency.

THE UNITED STATES rice industry has a problem. While consumption of rice is holding steady, imports keep rising. That means the domestic industry is losing market share.

There's a simple reason for the decline. A strategy change in Arkansas, the nation's largest producer of rice, caused the problem. The Arkansas rice producers moved to a variety of rice that could be milled more efficiently.

Only one problem: the variety that mills the most efficiently doesn't taste as good when it's cooked. Since most consumers know nothing about milling, but everything about taste, they have opted for other varieties, including more imported rice.

As one industry executive told me, it was yet

another case of efficiency winning out over effectiveness—with bad results.

It's hardly an isolated problem. A few years ago, Walmart ran into widespread problems when it launched a project to increase efficiency by eliminating slow-moving products. As the company quickly found out, cutting out too many products reduces customer appeal and, in short order, sales.

Efficiency is extremely important to competitiveness, profitability, and long-term growth. But pursuing efficiency at the cost of effectiveness can lead to declines in quality, service, and sales.

Defeat the Peter Principle.

THINK ABOUT THE best job you ever had. Most likely, you'll think about a great manager. Great managers make work interesting and important, find ways to grow the skills of their team members, and eliminate as many problems as possible.

When you think about the worst job you ever had, you probably think about a bad manager. They come in all shapes and sizes: those who micro-manage and make us feel incapable of even the smallest decisions; those who make no decisions and let chaos ensue. There are bad managers who foster a contentious environment, pitting co-workers against each other.

Too many workers are promoted to manager because of superior skills they demonstrated in a previous job. Sure, they are great at their tasks, but not so great at motivating others to be great. That's the essence of the Peter Principle—people promoted to their level of incompetence.

However, by continuing to learn, a manager can defeat the Peter Principle and rise even higher. Great managers require training to become great. That's why top companies spend so much time training managers, and top managers seek to improve themselves. It starts with remembering that clear communication means *listening* as well as talking. Success relies on creating a positive workplace, with clear goals and the tools needed to achieve those goals.

The better its managers perform, the better the company performs. And the less likely team members will leave a job due to a bad manager.

Speak the right language.

SHORTLY BEFORE THE 2014 World Cup competition, a Brazilian businessman I know asked me who I thought would win. I don't know much about soccer, but I do know how to irritate a Brazilian buddy.

Knowing the rivalries of South America, I named the team from Argentina, with star player Lionel Messi leading the way. He shook his head violently in disagreement and ran to a nearby wood panel . . . and then he knocked.

"Why did you do that?" I asked. He explained that in Brazil, knocking wood is a superstition to put a jinx on something else.

In the United States, we knock wood for a

completely different reason—to avoid jinxing ourselves. It's the same gesture, but Americans do it to protect themselves and Brazilians do it to impede someone else.

The growing complexity of today's business world means that we need to understand language and cultural nuances everywhere. We need to understand that exchanging business cards is anything but casual with a Japanese colleague. That shaking hands is a multiple-part ritual in Mexico.

And those differences aren't just between cultures, but also generations. That's why "California Girls" is a song by the Beach Boys for baby boomers, but not at all the same as "California Gurls" sung by Katy Perry.

You need to know something about the person you're doing business with or your words can fall flat or even worse.

Knock wood, because it could happen to you.

Accentuate the possible.

BILLY BEANE, THE general manager of the Oakland A's baseball team, is known for finding a way to get unusually high performance from his players. Beane's talents made him the subject of the book and movie *Moneyball*.

Beane understands that players can't simply run faster or throw harder. Instead, he uses players in specific situations that best employ their strengths and limit their weaknesses. For the A's, this means featuring hitters who have the best chance to succeed against specific pitchers.

The formula keeps producing a winner.

Business leaders need take a similarly unvarnished

look at their associates to understand strengths and weaknesses. It's why so many companies give personality tests like Myers-Briggs to better understand their teams. That kind of knowledge allows you to put your team—and your company—in a position to succeed.

Know when to break the limits.

SOMETIMES LIMITS ARE artificially created and destined to be shattered.

Roger Bannister was both a world-class runner and medical student in 1954. At the time, it was universally accepted that a human could not run a mile in less than four minutes. People thought a runner's heart would explode if he went that fast. Bannister thought that limit was absurd and set out to prove it wrong.

On May 6, 1954, Bannister did as he planned, breaking the so-called unbreakable barrier by six-tenths of a second. Just forty-six days later, another runner completed the mile in just under 3:58. The

current world record is 3:43!

Now relate this to your business. What limits are artificially placed on your business and the success of you and your colleagues? Embrace Bannister's lesson that some limits simply don't make sense and need shattering. Use this remarkable man's achievement as a rallying point to focus on breaking those limits.

Remember, whether you think you can or can't do something . . . you are already right. You can only do what you believe is possible.

Appeal to human nature.

YOU CAN'T SELL products to people without first understanding basic human behavior.

Murray Raphel, a noted business speaker, talked about Maslow's hierarchy of needs, a sociological theory of what makes people tick. Raphel reminded audiences of Maslow's lesson that once people satisfy their basic needs of food, clothing, and shelter, their desires change.

They want more—like love and acceptance. That's why membership clubs and loyalty cards work. People like the feeling of belonging and of being treated as if they are special. It's why thanking people by name when they use a credit card or check creates a special connection.

Business leaders need not be psychiatrists, but a

basic understanding of human nature is essential to sales success.

The best product designers and advertising people know how to use our basic traits to attract customers. Graphic designer and photographer Heather Long explains: "We are drawn to bright, shiny objects." When you show people an assortment of photographs, their eyes are always attracted to the brightest part of the photo.

Stand in the aisle of any supermarket and you can see this at work. It's why eye-popping colors dot so many packages. It draws our eye, and our money frequently follows.

It's simply human nature.

Focus on the basics.

THERE IS A simple way to lose weight. It doesn't involve any of the "miracle" cures you see on television or the Internet and it only takes two steps. Here they are:

- Exercise more
- Eat less

It's that simple. Still, there is a constant parade of new dieting strategies, guaranteed to work, but most likely will fail. The problem, according to Kim Kirchherr, a registered dietitian based near Chicago, is that most people want an easy solution, but better diets and more exercise are hard.

The same holds true for business. We all want success, which is why there are almost as many business books as there are diet guides. Yet with business as well as dieting, lasting success comes from bedrock values and hard work.

Successful businesses need to provide a distinct value that will convince buyers to select them. Building value requires good products, people, and services, competitive pricing, and a willingness to evolve with customer needs.

In other words, it's every bit as hard as losing weight.

Great ideas can be found nearby.

THE SINGER/SONGWRITER John Ondrasik jokes that he was an overnight success who took twenty years to get there.

Ondrasik is better known by his stage name, Five for Fighting, and his megahits "Superman" ("It's Not Easy") and "100 Years." In the wake of his first big hit he was afraid he would be remembered as a one-hit wonder. Determined to climb the charts again, he woke early every day to try out new songs, and in the process, serenaded his neighbor picking up the newspaper in the driveway.

Ondrasik has learned through the years that great ideas are out there if he remembers to listen.

He tells how one of his children looked at him one day and said, "I just love you." The line stuck with him, and a few months later he had a song by that very name at number twenty-four on the adult contemporary charts.

Business history is full of great ideas that were hanging out there until someone listened. Baby food pioneer Frank Gerber was responding to his wife's need for an easier way to feed a newborn. Alexander Graham Bell's desire to build a better hearing aid for his wife led to his work on the telephone.

Michael Kittredge was trying to make a gift for his mother. The result of his work was a scented candle that grew into the Yankee Candle Company.

We have to look and listen, because great ideas are everywhere—even right at home.

Great ideas can be found far away.

COKE ZERO SEEMED like a can't-miss idea—a low-calorie soft drink targeted at men. But a few months after its introduction, the product just would not catch on.

Mel Landis, chief retail sales officer for Coca-Cola, says the outlook was bleak until the company noticed a very different picture of performance far, far away—in Australia, where Coke Zero was becoming a hit.

The only difference between the Australia effort and the rest of the world: down under, the product came in a black can. Everywhere else, the can was white. Coke was running many tests on the new

product to learn what worked and didn't work.

Just like that, Coke Zero was switched to a black can worldwide, and today it is a billion-dollar brand.

This idea can work for any size company: keep your eyes on the horizon. You might find someone solving a problem you have or addressing an opportunity you never knew existed.

We have to look and listen, because great ideas are everywhere—even across the globe.

Embrace criticism.

THERE'S A RULE of thumb: for every complaint you receive, there are forty-nine other customers unhappy about the same thing. It's a rule that's impossible to prove, but you should never ignore it.

Because here's the thing about those forty-nine customers—instead of complaining to you, they may have just stopped doing business with you.

Complaints are gold. Taken properly, negative comments point out a clear direction for improvement.

Like politicians who only talk to voter groups and media outlets that share their beliefs, too many businesses today are only interested in getting approval, not complaints.

Numerous businesses ask you to take a survey about them and urge you to give them the top rating. Their salespeople explain that their jobs are dependent on getting the highest ratings possible. But you don't usually have an outstanding experience with your auto mechanic or restaurant. Those businesses would learn a whole lot more if they asked you to highlight one area needing improvement, rather than beg you to give the highest rating.

Ask your customers what you're doing wrong—so you can fix it.

Hire for attitude.

WHAT FOLLOWS IS an actual help wanted ad that ran on Facebook:

> *"If you live, breathe, and even some-*
> *times dream about making customers*
> *smile, SAGE has an opening for a full*
> *time position for someone with a great*
> *work ethic and an appreciation of*
> *outstanding customer service. We believe*
> *that a good fit for this position is a col-*
> *lege graduate (recent or not so recent)*
> *who is currently under-employed, with*
> *a passion for both personal and company*

growth. The position does not require
technical expertise, but does require a
desire to learn about the technology that
SAGE supports. Initial job duties will
be clerical and administrative with
expected growth to technical services or
sales & marketing. Ask about our hot
lunch program."

Chances are, you had no inkling what SAGE does until you read the third-to-last sentence. That tells you something amazing. Here is a technical services company demonstrating what every good manager knows about hiring the best people—you can teach skills, but you can't teach attitude.

Think about the help wanted ads you run and whether they would lure a talented employee away from SAGE. Worse yet, would your current staff think of leaving you if they read this ad?

A clever help wanted ad says plenty to potential employees. It sets the tone of the company—in this case, a workplace where the priority is clearly customer service. This ad conveys a sense that SAGE is a great place to work, a place to learn new skills and grow.

Oh, yes, and I may be getting terrific free lunches. Where do I sign up?

Share your secrets.

IN SO MANY ways, it was a shocking announcement. In June 2014, Elon Musk, the CEO of Tesla Motors, publicly released all the patented technology that makes Tesla electric cars so special.

In essence, Musk took his competitive advantage and gave it away. Forget the awards and praise heaped on Tesla Motors, he basically said. Now *you* can build it, too.

And that "you" meant Toyota, General Motors, and other car companies. It was a real head-scratching move . . . or was it?

Musk is following a strategy to build both his category—electric cars—and his brand.

Currently, the size of the electric car market is minuscule, which means owners run into widespread

problems ranging from a lack of charging stations to a lack of repair know-how. By releasing the patents, that situation could change, and in a few years, the number of electric cars on the road could significantly increase. Tesla makes what many experts say is both the best electric car and the best car overall, so Musk stands to gain a great deal if the category builds.

If your business is in a new category or is simply pushing into a new flavor or variety, take a tip from Elon Musk: grow the category to grow your brand.

Make the sale.

AS SOMEONE WHO runs a small family nursery, Amanda Shenstone might be excused for having a slightly offbeat business philosophy. Graceful Gardens of Mecklenburg, New York, the nursery Shenstone runs with her husband, has all the makings of the kind of business most of us think of as one step up from a hobby.

But Shenstone is in business to make money. Asked to name the most important aspect of her business, Shenstone barely hesitates before saying: getting people to buy!

That's a traditional business goal, but it's as important to Graceful Gardens as it is to IBM. Getting customers to make purchases is key for every business.

No matter what your business, the ultimate goal is to sell your products or services to customers and to do it so well that they come back again and again. Every day, you have to reinforce the special aspects of your business and start the game once more.

Shenstone is a great example. To emphasize the local nature of their business, she and her husband are regulars at the nearby Ithaca Farmers' Market. They also do a significant business online. The Graceful Gardens website emphasizes everything that's important to the business: low prices, advice on how to care for plants, garden design tips, shipping information, and the story of the owners.

All of it reinforces who they are, what they do, and why you should buy.

Pay attention to changing demographics.

WHEN ASKED WHY he robbed banks, Willie Sutton reportedly said: "That's where the money is."

In business, that means learning to serve the Hispanic community, the largest minority group in the United States. Terry Soto of About Marketing has spent her career helping companies understand how to do business with the Hispanic community. She says there are four myths to dispel.

Myth 1: *They are all immigrants.*

Fact: Nearly two-thirds of Hispanics are native-born Americans, and the native-born Hispanic population will outpace the immigrant population from now on. And keep this in mind: 800,000 Hispanic children will turn eighteen every year for the foreseeable future. That's a huge number of potential customers and associates.

Myth 2: *They don't speak English.*
Fact: Two-thirds of all Hispanics in the United States speak English. Many families live in multigenerational homes where someone fluent in English assists on shopping trips. Of course, if you want to create a welcoming experience, it pays to offer bilingual options.

Myth 3: *Hispanics shop very differently than Anglos.*
Fact: There are some specific items Hispanics buy in larger quantities than other cultural groups, and they have certain cultural needs for holidays and celebrations that can be different. But for the most part, Hispanics buy the same basic products as everyone else. Like all shoppers, they seek convenience and good prices.

Myth 4: *The longer they are in the United States, the more their tastes will change.*
Fact: This happens to some extent with all immigrant groups, but Soto says that Hispanics will always hang on to elements of their culture. Respect those elements, and you can form a lasting and profitable relationship.

Go where the money is. That certainly includes the Hispanic demographic.

Have a succession plan.

BUSINESS LEADERS ARE paid to think about the unthinkable. One unthinkable event that should be on the agenda: death.

Surely, it's the most uncomfortable topic of discussion. No one wants to consider his or her own mortality, but there are critical decisions to be made. That's why we have wills and life insurance—in case the worst happens. It should be obvious that companies need the same type of plans.

The good news is that many do. Companies have rules on how many executives can fly together on a single plane to avoid a management catastrophe. Some have specific succession plans to deal with any tragedy.

There's one midwestern retailer that requires each CEO to write and update a regular letter to his/her successor. The letter begins: "In the case of my sudden demise . . ."

But death isn't the only motivation behind succession planning. People retire, move to new jobs, and get promoted all the time. Companies and teams with clear succession plans avoid the confusion and internal battles that can follow any such event. (For a quick history lesson, look at the executive exodus that followed the retirement of General Electric's legendary leader Jack Welch. Uncertainty is never a friend.)

Many companies push managers at all levels to constantly think about their bench strength and to clearly identify, train, and groom a replacement. Such discussions need to be done with positive intent: after all, you can't promote one manager if a replacement isn't ready to step in.

Everyone needs an umbrella. You don't know when it will happen, but you know that one day it's going to rain.

Update your rulebook.

THE ODDS ARE pretty good that the first business game we all played was Monopoly. I never really liked the game. My sister was older, stronger, and smarter than me, which meant that she'd always win big at Monopoly. The game usually ended with someone kicking the board, sending the houses and hotels flying.

Now Monopoly is schooling us again. Hasbro, the game's owner, recently made the most modern of moves for the aged game.

Hasbro is well aware that many Monopoly players have their own house rules that pass through family generations. In a nod to modern times, Hasbro is allowing players to post some of those house rules on its Facebook page. Hasbro will allow others to vote for their favorite house rules, which will be added to the game guide in 2015.

Frequently, updating the rulebook is exactly what it takes to succeed. Whether it's Major League Baseball adopting instant replay or Microsoft making the Office suite of programs available free for tablets, the recognition of reality spurs these changes. Baseball understands that it needs to incorporate technology because fans watching on high-definition televisions have already done so. And Microsoft understands that tablets and smartphones, not desktops and laptops, are the future.

No one—not even Hasbro—owns a monopoly.

Keep getting better.

THE FIRST TIME I shaved, back in the early 1970s, my dad's razor scared me. It was a Gillette single-blade safety razor, though frankly, I could see nothing safe in it. It was little more than a sharpened sliver of metal, held by a heavy handle. But it was safer than the razor my dad had started shaving with thirty years earlier.

Luckily for me, time and razors marched on. I progressed through the Trac II, Atra, Mach 3, and, briefly, disposable Bic shavers. I bought in as the heads got more flexible, as lubricating strips were added, and as vibrating handles became the fashion.

Each time I tried a new razor, I had the same feeling: this is the best shave ever. With each new innovation the process felt safer. I couldn't imagine it improving any more until I used the Gillette Fusion. And as of this writing, a new version of the Fusion has just come out, and I know that my shaving experience will get better still.

Gillette is the unmatched king of its category for a very good reason. Even as the company, now a division of Proctor & Gamble, launches the best razor ever, it continues working on the device that will eventually replace it. Forget the old adage, "If it ain't broke, don't fix it." Gillette doesn't wait for anything to break—it just keeps fixing.

Gillette isn't the only company with a fixation of pushing the boundaries of its products. There are the endless improvements of smartphones or running shoes for other examples.

True business leaders never stop improving themselves and their products. That is how they stay on top.

Be authentic.

TODAY'S CONSUMERS ARE never more than a few Google clicks away from learning all kinds of things about your business. More than ever, companies must recognize that nothing is secret.

This is the age of transparency and authenticity, which means your company has to live by a cleaner code of conduct than ever before. Whatever you do and whatever you support, someone is always watching.

Positions taken by the owners of Hobby Lobby on employee health benefits and Chick-fil-A on same sex marriage have caused those businesses to gain and lose customers. In both those cases, fans rallied to support the businesses and others protested.

Transparency also puts newfound pressure on companies to live by the business values they trumpet. Many supermarkets sell organic products, but it's unlikely that any other food retailer faces the pressure that Whole Foods has to uphold its standards on organic products. Likewise, customers found it easy to embarrass Subway by demonstrating with photographs and rulers that its foot-long sandwiches measured only eleven inches.

When your message and behavior is authentic, people know, and when it isn't, they'll tell others.

Learn new tricks.

A FEW YEARS back, professional hockey player Jeff Halpern felt his career slipping away. After ten years in the National Hockey League, his statistics were growing weaker.

Not willing to ease into retirement, Halpern did something almost unheard of for a professional athlete: he started taking skating lessons. For Halpern, that meant hitting the rink with his coach at 6:00 a.m.

That was in 2010. As of 2014, Halpern is still in the NHL, and, according to experts, skating better than ever. Apparently, even an aging professional athlete can improve his skills.

Businesspeople need do the same. Consider how much technology has changed during your career.

Nearly every professional needs to learn new skills, whether it's the newest version of Microsoft Office, how to work an upgraded cell phone, or harnessing the power of social media. Learning new skills will help you and your company grow.

Without constant improvement, you could be skating on thin ice.

Smile and the world smiles with you.

CRITICS ARE ALL around these days, powered by social media, to point out the flaws of your business, your people, and your products. So more than ever, business people need to know how to respond.

How about smiling?

No one wants public criticism, but knowing how to handle difficult situations with a sense of humor can turn a negative into a positive. The range of responses can be extraordinary.

For example, there's a restaurant in Washington, DC, that for months has posted a sign inviting patrons to try a dish that "one Yelp reviewer said was the worst they had in their life." By featuring the negative review so prominently, the restaurant successfully makes people chuckle. In fact, the sign is building business.

A few years back, Janet Riley, an executive at the American Meat Institute, was asked to appear on Jon Stewart's *Daily Show* for a story on hot dog ingredients. A consumer group was arguing that hot dogs needed cigarette-style warnings. It had all the makings of a disaster, but Riley was ready. She understood the sardonic nature of the show and met it head on, joking about her job and referring to herself as the Queen of Wien (as in *wieners.*) Riley came off as clearly in on the joke. She got her laughs and, more importantly, made her points on behalf of her industry on a show that millions rate as their top source of news.

When you keep your sense of humor, you often have the last laugh.

Deliver great experiences.

THE LATE POET Maya Angelou said, "I've learned that people will forget what you said, people will forget what you did, but people will never forget how you made them feel."

Making the customer or co-worker feel great is an essential part of business success.

Everyone can remember a time a business interaction turned terrible because our knowledge or position was belittled. It could have happened across a negotiation table or a lunch counter. Conversely, we remember pleasant moments, too: when a clerk complimented our taste or a colleague praised our work.

The customer experience comes at every point where customers interact with your company's products or people. And it works for any kind of business. Every trip I make to a simple In-N-Out burger stand is always enhanced by the smiling person taking my order. In contrast, my recent stay at the Waldorf-Astoria was marred by an absurdly long wait to check in.

For your customers and clients, it's the great experience that keeps them coming back.

Don't rest on your laurels.

AT THE HEIGHT of the Roman Empire, returning generals would be greeted with both a celebration and a reminder that their fame was fleeting. In Latin: *Sic transit gloria mundi*, or "Thus passes the glory of the world."

Kjell Nordstrom, a Swedish economist, is fond of reminding business audiences of the temporary nature of competitive advantage. As Nordstrom explains, businesses achieve significant gains when they find a new way to serve a market or do something that no one else can do.

But those advantages are only temporary. After that, competition catches up and the only competitive advantage becomes efficiencies that produce lower prices. The challenge businesses face, of course, is to constantly create new temporary advantages.

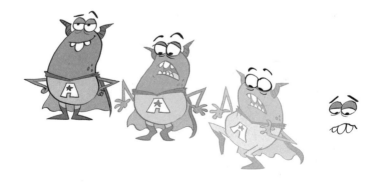

There are exceptions. The rare company finds a way to do something so unique that even after years of operation, others still struggle to catch up. Nordstrom's favorite example is Ikea, the seventy-year-old Swedish furniture and home goods store.

Nordstrom acknowledges that many shoppers don't like visiting Ikea. The store has even been ridiculed on the television show *30 Rock*. Sure, the prices are good and the furniture fairly durable, but the shopping trip is arduous.

Nordstrom says there's a simple test: "When people say they don't want to go to Ikea, what's the alternative? In essence, there is none." In other words, Ikea's temporary advantage continues.

That's a victory even a Roman general would admire.

Learn to juggle.

IN A FAMOUS episode of *I Love Lucy*, the star has a job on a candy assembly line. Lucy handles her task easily when the candy comes at a slow and steady pace, but when it picks up, comedy mayhem ensues.

For most of us, that moment of mayhem is anything but funny. Learning to juggle demands or react to sped-up demands is essential for every job from receptionist to CEO. We need to learn a range of the basic skills that dominate most of our time and be ready for those hard moments when everything comes into play at once.

Craig Mulcahy, principal trombonist for the National Symphony Orchestra and a professor at the University of Maryland, says music performance offers a great example of juggling. "There's so much to focus on at one time. It all needs to be done at a high and consistent level to achieve success," he says. Concert musicians need to track their fellow musicians, the pace around them, and the conductor's commands, all without missing a beat. Minus that ability, Mulcahy knows his students will struggle to succeed in an orchestra.

Office workers know the drill. There are times they have two or more projects with top priority, a request for a meeting, a ringing phone, and a constant flow of e-mails. Suddenly they are like Lucy on the assembly line.

Juggling requires prioritizing and a keen understanding of how to move quickly from one skill to the next. Good managers help associates set priorities and recognize when help is needed.

Otherwise the juggling pins fall on the floor.

Measure what's important.

BUSINESS RELIES ON numbers. Numbers help us gauge performance, tell us how well we are performing, and frequently point out problems.

But numbers can paint a misleading picture. When tracking numbers, be sure you measure the *right* things.

A few years back, a national retailer told me that store managers used to be evaluated on simply sales, profits, and costs. Then the company made a startling discovery. They found that the best manager isn't always in the highest performing store. The best manager could be in a poor-performing unit that ekes out a profit despite the store's tough market conditions, competition, and other difficulties. In contrast, the manager of a high-performing unit might benefit

from all kinds of good fortune, and might not have the skills to get all he/she should from the store.

In other words, a company needs to measure performance versus potential.

Consider all the factors that determine success and failure in your business and measure accordingly. While numbers may not lie, they can certainly mislead.

Set goals.

IF YOU DON'T know where you're going, any road
can get you there. Your CEO should set clear goals
to guide your company.

In a 2014 interview with *Forbes*, Denise Morrison,
CEO of Campbell Soup, talked about goals for herself and her company.

Morrison always considered how her individual
steps would lead to her career goal of running a large
company. She asked herself, "What skills and com-
petencies do you need along the way to be great at
that?" She recognized that "you will make different
decisions about the assignments you take, and it's not

all about titles and ladders and layers. It's about skills and experiences."

As CEO, she has specific goals for her company that guide her steps. She wants to build courage and better decision making into the Campbell culture, to foster risk taking, innovation, and speed to market. But to make that happen, she knows she needs to demonstrate her commitment to the goal.

That's the reason for some major personnel moves she's made since she became CEO in 2011, bringing in outsiders to run marketing, international, and research and development. As Morrison says, if a leader doesn't show the way, no one will follow.

That way is always in the direction of specific goals.

Be important.

BERRY GORDY JR., the founder of Motown Records, used a simple question to determine if a song would be released. Gordy would ask, "If you had only enough money to buy this record or buy a sandwich, which would you choose?"

The point was simple: each song needed to be so great that a listener would forego a meal to get it. It must have been a pretty good filter, given the number of superstar groups and recordings produced by Motown.

Is your product or service important enough to drive customer action?

Think of Gordy's question with a twist for today:

if you only had four minutes to relax, would you spend it with this song or on Twitter? What matters more to your customer?

Your business must produce products or services that matter enough for people to plunk down hard-earned money for them.

Be important to your customers.

Create value.

LOW PRICE IS not a synonym for value.

Value is constantly changing, depending on how a consumer views a specific product or experience. Value is the reason for behaviors that seem contradictory, but actually make sense.

As consumers, we select certain products based primarily on price. Given a choice between two neighboring gas stations, it's hard to imagine most people selecting the higher-priced alternative. But those same consumers will gladly shell out extra money for other liquids at Starbucks, because they perceive they are receiving value for their dollar.

Value is a complex equation determined by individual customer factors that can include (but are not

Super Value

limited to): history with a product, health needs, convenience, company policies, shipping costs, and price.

Even economically distressed shoppers look for value. They understand that rock-bottom pricing means nothing if the product they buy doesn't last or satisfy basic needs. That's why most merchants emphasize quality in their value-focused private label products.

Understand the value equation that customers bring to you. And then satisfy the daylights out of that.

Anticipate customer needs.

SOME OF THE greatest successes in business have come from companies solving problems that customers never knew they had. Improving transportation in the late 1800s meant finding faster horses until they invented the automobile.

Not so long ago, you couldn't listen to your own music selections while walking, jogging, or riding in airplanes. Before iPods and all the devices to follow, there was the Walkman, Sony's ingenious personal music device. Once introduced, everyone had to have a portable personal music player.

People always have unmet needs, and great companies keep finding a way to identify and solve them.

For example, look at today's new safety advances in cars. Because drivers are increasingly distracted—probably by their personal devices—cars now feature sophisticated warning systems that alert drivers to all kinds of danger. Follow the car ahead of you too closely or drift into another lane without signaling, and your car alerts you. In many cars, the driver doesn't have any control over the headlights. Soon, we may not need the driver at all.

Sometimes the fix involves much less sophistication. It can be laundry detergent that works in any temperature. Or movie theaters with cup holders for our soft drinks.

Smart companies figure out what customers really want before customers know they have a problem.

Keep your foundation strong.

FOR CUSTOMERS, BUSINESSES are simply what
they see. When they want clothes they go to a clothing store, for food, to a supermarket. They don't care
how the products got to the destination, just that
they are there.

Businesses, however, should never forget the
things a customer *doesn't* see. The foundation of a
good business includes technology, distribution systems, and personnel policies.

Consider the usually unsexy topic of logistics.
Without a cutting-edge distribution system, consumers would never find all those items waiting to
be purchased. Worse yet, a sloppy or out-of-date distribution system is usually fatal. If your competition
moves products through its systems better than you,
it can offer lower prices and greater variety.

Great logistics have been essential to many businesses. Logistics fueled Walmart's stunning rise to retail dominance. It's how Zara offers cutting-edge fashion at competitive prices. And it's why so many companies today worry about Amazon.

Customer service and product mix are what the customers see. But neglect logistics, technology, and all those important foundational steps, and your business will collapse.

Don't let success ruin you.

SUCCESS IS BOTH our goal and our enemy.

It's our goal for obvious reasons. Success means we are doing things right. We are serving clients, beating the competition, and moving ahead. Success is a place that merits celebrations with our staff, reflection on what we are doing right, and joy.

But success can also be our enemy. The world around us is constantly changing. What was good enough yesterday is frequently not good enough tomorrow. We work long hours looking for an edge, trying to achieve success. But that achievement is fleeting because the status quo is never enough.

Far too many once-successful companies have failed for not changing with the times. High-ranking companies like Kodak, Beatrice, Nabisco, Honeywell, and United Technologies have been absorbed by

others, shrunk considerably, or disappeared entirely.

History shows many companies that no longer exist or survive only as pieces of new companies. None of these businesses meant to follow a downward course. But the world around them changed and they failed to find a new way to succeed.

Remember, evolution is survival of the fittest, not the largest or strongest.

Evolve.

WHY HAVEN'T SCIENTISTS solved the problem of food-borne illness? Despite all the scientific measures we've taken, killer bacteria keeps popping up in various meats, vegetables, and other foods. Likewise, every year the flu keeps coming back.

Jill Hollingsworth, a doctor of veterinary medicine who has worked on some of the largest food safety issues in the United States, says the reason is simple. The bugs evolve. In order to survive, they find a way to overcome whatever measures are taken to prevent them. In some cases they even get stronger, which is why doctors always express such concern about patients misusing antibiotics.

Turns out that germs, viruses, and bacteria

provide a great metaphor for business. Everything evolves and everything changes. Competition always finds a new way to survive and customer needs shift to new places. The status quo is in flux all the time.

The world is full of companies that demonstrate the power of constant evolution. Toyota, once considered a manufacturer of sub-standard cars, became the hallmark of product excellence, creating Lexus for upscale drivers, Scion for new drivers, and Prius for environmental concerns. Heinz took its staid old ketchup and added colors, flavors, ironic labels, and even a complete redesign of the iconic bottle—all to change with the times.

Even the strongest and most powerful businesses and most capable businesspeople need to constantly change or risk being left behind.

It's a simple truth of nature from the smallest beings among us.

Break the rules.

RULE BREAKERS ARE known by many names: innovators, inventors, and disrupters.

Legend has it that in building Walmart, Sam Walton would make lists of all the things he seemingly could not do, such as creating a new pricing model or locating large stores in small communities—and then he did them. Steve Jobs broke countless rules by making computers easy for anyone to use, then turning phones into miniature computers. And Jeff Bezos of Amazon continues to break rules by attempting to bring any product to any shopper wherever they might be.

Rules are important. Rules give us guidelines and boundaries. From rules, we learn what's been done well in the past and how to move toward a successful future. Rules should be followed—most of the time.

But rules can be especially useful when you know it's time to break them.

YOU GOTTA KNOW THE
Rules!

Animation Rules!
by Steve Hickner

Customer Service Rules!
by Don Gallegos

Business Rules!
by Michael Sansolo

Retail Rules!
by Kevin Coupe

AVAILABLE 2015

Supermarket Rules!   Marketing Rules!
Feedback Rules!   Customer Experience Rules!

To browse our entire collection of **Rules!** books, visit
www.therulesbooks.com

Also by Michael Sansolo

$14.95
ISBN: 978-0-9711542-8-5
211 pp.

Movies are magical. They are wonderful releases from the stresses of everyday life. But movies also contain valuable lessons you can use in your business life.

In their very entertaining book, *The Big Picture: Essential Business Lessons From the Movies*, authors Kevin Coupe and Michael Sansolo show how you can use the stories in movies to solve problems in your business life. From *The Godfather* to *Tootsie*, from *The Wedding Singer* to *Babe*, you'll see how your favorite movies have important lessons about customer service, leadership, planning, and more.

Available at
www.brigantinemedia.com